D1716377

SAUROPHAGANAX

and Other Meat-Eating Dinosaurs

by **Dougal Dixon**

illustrated by **Steve Weston and James Field**

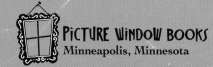

PICTURE WINDOW BOOKS
Minneapolis, Minnesota

Picture Window Books
151 Good Counsel Drive
P.O. Box 669
Mankato, MN 56002-0669
877-845-8392
www.picturewindowbooks.com

Library of Congress Cataloging-in-Publication Data
Dixon, Dougal.
Saurophaganax and other meat-eating dinosaurs
/ by Dougal Dixon ; illustrated by Steve Weston and
James Field.
p. cm. — (Dinosaur Find)
Includes index.
ISBN 978-1-4048-5180-1 (library binding)
1. Dinosaurs—Juvenile literature. 2. Dinosaurs—
Food—Juvenile literature. 3. Predatory animals—
Juvenile literature. I. Weston, Steve, ill. II. Field, James,
1959- ill. III. Title.
QE861.5.D6476 2009
567.912—dc22   2008043363

Acknowledgments
This book was produced for Picture Window Books
by Bender Richardson White, U.K.

Illustrations by James Field (cover and pages 4–5, 9,
13, 17, 21) and Steve Weston (pages 7, 11, 15, 19).
Diagrams by Stefan Chabluk.

Photographs: iStockphotos pages 6 (Jonathan
Heger), 8 (Mark Kostich), 10 (Peter Miller), 12
(Steve Lovegrove), 14 (David T Gomez), 16 (Klaas
Lingbeek- van Kranen), 18 (John Pitcher), 20
(Kristian Sekulic).

Consultant: John Stidworthy, Scientific Fellow of
the Zoological Society, London, and former
Lecturer in the Education Department, Natural
History Museum, London.

Types of dinosaurs

In the Dinosaur Find books,
a red shape at the top of a
left-hand page shows the
animal was a meat-eater.
A green shape shows it was
a plant-eater.

Just how big—or small— were they?

Dinosaurs were many different
sizes. We have compared their
size to one of the following:

 Chicken
2 feet (60 centimeters) tall
Weight 6 pounds (2.7 kilograms)

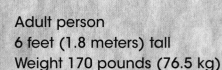 Adult person
6 feet (1.8 meters) tall
Weight 170 pounds (76.5 kg)

 Elephant
10 feet (3 m) tall
Weight 12,000 pounds
(5,400 kg)

TABLE OF CONTENTS

WHAT'S INSIDE?

Dinosaurs! These meat-eating dinosaurs lived between 230 million and 65 million years ago. They hunted other dinosaurs for food. Find out how they lived and what they have in common with today's animals.

3

LIFE AS A MEAT-EATER

Dinosaurs lived between 230 million and 65 million years ago. The world did not look the same then. Much of the land and many of the seas were not in the same places as today. Herds of huge plant-eating dinosaurs roamed the lands, and there were also meat-eating dinosaurs that hunted them.

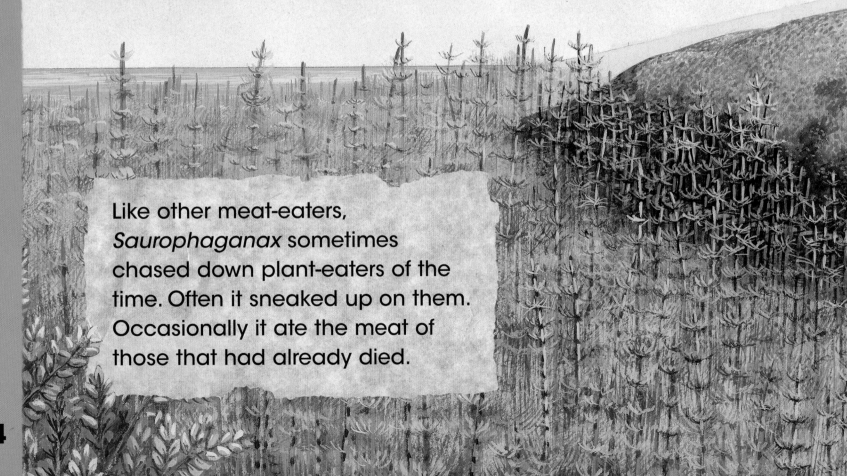

Like other meat-eaters, *Saurophaganax* sometimes chased down plant-eaters of the time. Often it sneaked up on them. Occasionally it ate the meat of those that had already died.

DASPLETOSAURUS

Pronunciation:
das-PLEET-o-SAW-rus

What could be scarier than *Daspletosaurus,* one of the fiercest meat-eating dinosaurs that ever lived? A whole pack of them! *Daspletosaurus* moved around in family packs, hunting and killing the big plant-eating dinosaurs of the time.

Pack hunters today

Modern lions hunt and kill in family groups, just as *Daspletosaurus* did in the Age of Dinosaurs.

Size Comparison

A number of *Daspletosaurus* fed on the body of a single plant-eating dinosaur such as *Triceratops*.

SAUROPHAGANAX

Pronunciation:
SAW-ro-FAG-an-ax

Saurophaganax was the biggest meat-eater of its time. Even so, it would have thought twice about attacking the biggest of the plant-eaters. A healthy adult *Apatosaurus* was just too big to be killed by *Saurophaganax*.

Careful hunters today

A modern tiger will not attack a fully grown elephant, just as *Saurophaganax* was once careful not to hunt the largest plant-eaters of its time.

Size Comparison

Sometimes *Saurophaganax* was able to stalk and kill a young, old, or weak *Apatosaurus*.

Wrinkle-faced *Rugops* was one of the largest meat-eating dinosaurs. It was too big and heavy to do much hunting. It probably spent most of its time eating dinosaurs that had already died.

Scavengers today

The modern hyena sometimes eats animals that have already been killed, like *Rugops* did long ago.

Size Comparison

Natural disasters, such as floods, killed many dinosaurs. Big meat-eaters like *Rugops* would find plenty to eat among the flood victims.

Some of the big meat-eating dinosaurs could swim across rivers. *Tyrannotitan* was one of them. Sometimes it stayed in the water, sneaking up on herds of big plant-eating dinosaurs. Then *Tyrannotitan* could attack.

Sneaky hunters today

Big crocodiles wait in shallow waters. Then they leap up and catch animals that have come to drink, much like *Tyrannotitan* may have once done.

Size Comparison

Tyrannotitan had a crocodile-like tail. The tail could have helped it swim across rivers and lakes.

GIGANTORAPTOR

Pronunciation:
JIH-gan-toe-RAP-tor

Gigantoraptor looked different from the other big meat-eating dinosaurs. With its long legs, flexible neck, and beak, the dinosaur looked more like a giant bird. With its powerful legs, *Gigantoraptor* could chase down small, fast animals.

Long-legged hunters today

The modern secretary bird can fly, but it prefers to hunt on the ground, like *Gigantoraptor* once did.

Size Comparison

When *Gigantoraptor* caught prey, it grabbed the animal with clawed hands. Then *Gigantoraptor* tore the prey to pieces with its beak.

15

DEINOCHEIRUS

Pronunciation:
dy-no-KY-rus

Deinocheirus had the longest arms of any of the meat-eating dinosaurs. Perhaps it used the long arms and huge claws to tear at prey. But it also used the long arms to pull down branches and eat leaves.

Plant-eating meat-eaters today

The modern panda belongs to the meat-eating group of mammals. However, it eats mostly plants as *Deinocheirus* may have done long ago.

Size Comparison

Deinocheirus stood on its hind legs to eat leaves from tall trees. It may have fed on leaves, insects, and other small animals.

MAPUSAURUS

Pronunciation:
MA-poo-SAW-rus

The biggest meat-eating dinosaur of what is now South America was *Mapusaurus*. The dinosaur was so big that it could attack and kill *Argentinosaurus*, the heaviest plant-eater of the time.

Biggest meat-eater today

The modern polar bear is one of the largest meat-eaters, just as *Mapusaurus* once was.

Size Comparison

Mapusaurus used its big teeth for killing. The dinosaur could raise its head to reach the neck of an *Argentinosaurus*. It killed by biting.

CRYOLOPHOSAURUS

Pronunciation:
CRY-o-LO-fo-SAW-rus

Some meat-eating dinosaurs had a highly decorated head. *Cryolophosaurus* had a jagged crest that ran sideways across its skull. The animal must have looked big when it was showing off to another *Cryolophosaurus*.

Head ornaments today

The modern male lion has a great shaggy mane. It uses the mane to show how big and strong it is, much like *Cryolophosaurus* did long ago.

Size Comparison

Cryolophosaurus' crest was brightly colored. It could be seen from far away.

21

WHERE DID THEY GO?

Dinosaurs are extinct, which means that none of them are alive today. Scientists study rocks and fossils to find clues about what happened to dinosaurs.

People have different explanations about what happened. Some people think a huge asteroid that hit Earth caused all sorts of climate changes, which caused the dinosaurs to die. Others think volcanic eruptions caused the climate change and that killed the dinosaurs. No one knows for sure what happened to all of the dinosaurs.

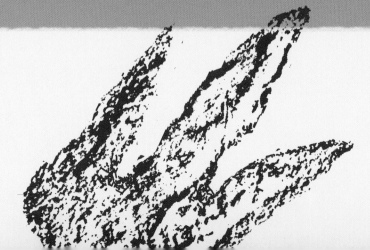

GLOSSARY

claws—tough, usually curved fingernails or toenails

crest—a structure on top of the head, usually used to signal to other animals

herd—a large group of animals that move, feed, and sleep together

packs—groups of animals that hunt and kill together

stalk—to follow when hunting

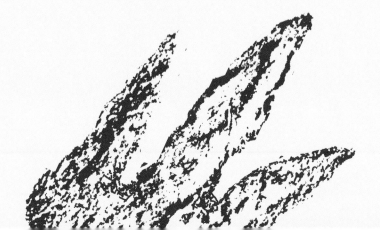

To Learn More

More Books to Read

Clark, Neil, and William Lindsay. *1001 Facts About Dinosaurs.* New York: Dorling Kindersley, 2002.

Dixon, Dougal. *Dougal Dixon's Amazing Dinosaurs.* Honesdale, Pa.: Boyds Mills Press, 2007.

Holtz, Thomas R., and Michael Brett-Surman. *Jurassic Park Institute Dinosaur Field Guide.* New York: Random House, 2001.

On the Web

FactHound offers a safe, fun way to find educator-approved Internet sites related to this book.

Here's what you do:
1. Visit *www.facthound.com*
2. Choose your grade level.
3. Begin your search.

This book's ID number is 9781404851801

Index

Look for other books in the Dinosaur Find series:

Bambiraptor and Other Feathered Dinosaurs

Baryonyx and Other Dinosaurs of the Isle of Wight Digs in England

Camarasaurus and Other Dinosaurs of the Garden Park Digs in Colorado

Chungkingosaurus and Other Plated Dinosaurs

Deinocheirus and Other Big, Fierce Dinosaurs

Diceratops and Other Horned Dinosaurs

Iguanodon and Other Leaf-Eating Dinosaurs

Mahakala and Other Insect-Eating Dinosaurs

Masiakasaurus and Other Fish-Eating Dinosaurs

Pawpawsaurus and Other Armored Dinosaurs

Torosaurus and Other Dinosaurs of the Badlands Digs in Montana

Xiaosaurus and Other Dinosaurs of the Dashanpu Digs in China